GAMES
you can BUILD
YOURSELF

By KATHARINA ZECHLIN

STERLING PUBLISHING CO., INC. NEW YORK
Oak Tree Press Co., Ltd. London & Sydney

Little Craft Book Series

Aluminum and Copper Tooling
Animating Films without a Camera
Appliqué and Reverse Appliqué
Balsa Wood Modelling
Bargello Stitchery
Beads Plus Macramé
Beauty Recipes from Natural Foods
Big-Knot Macramé
Candle-Making
Cellophane Creations
Ceramics by Slab
Coloring Papers
Corn-Husk Crafts
Corrugated Carton Crafting
Costumes from Crepe Paper
Crafting with Nature's Materials
Creating from Remnants
Creating Silver Jewelry with Beads
Creating with Beads
Creating with Burlap
Creating with Flexible Foam
Creating with Sheet Plastic
Creative Lace-Making with Thread and Yarn
Cross Stitchery

Curling, Coiling and Quilling
Decoupage—Simple and Sophisticated
Embossing of Metal (Repoussage)
Enamel without Heat
Felt Crafting
Finger Weaving: Indian Braiding
Flower Pressing
Folding Table Napkins
Games You Can Build Yourself
Greeting Cards You Can Make
Hooked and Knotted Rugs
Horseshoe-Nail Crafting
How to Add Designer Touches to Your Wardrobe
Ideas for Collage
Junk Sculpture
Lacquer and Crackle
Leathercrafting
Macramé
Make Your Own Elegant Jewelry
Making Paper Flowers
Making Picture Frames
Making Shell Flowers
Masks
Metal and Wire Sculpture

Model Boat Building
Monster Masks
Nail Sculpture
Needlepoint Simplified
Net-Making and Knotting
Off-Loom Weaving
Organic Jewelry You Can Ma
Patchwork and Other Quiltin
Pictures without a Camera
Potato Printing
Puppet-Making
Repoussage
Scissorscraft
Scrimshaw
Sculpturing with Wax
Sewing without a Pattern
Starting with Stained Glass
Stone Grinding and Polishing
String Things You Can Create
Tissue Paper Creations
Tole Painting
Trapunto: Decorative Quiltin
Whittling and Wood Carving

Translated by Manly Banister
Adapted by Burton Hobson

Contents

Games are Fun

Everyone enjoys playing games—they relax you when pressure builds up and they help to pass your leisure hours in a pleasant, constructive way. In many games, luck alone is not enough—you must use your head to devise a plan, even a trick or two, to outplay your opponent (or beat your own record if it is a game for one person).

How much more fun it is to build your game yourself! The planning, construction and decoration are a kind of game in themselves. And you will derive the satisfaction of having created something yourself.

Using the ideas in this book as a springboard, you can let your own personality and feelings show through in your choice of colors and designs. The game itself becomes a work of art—something you can enjoy just displayed on a table or stand, or hanging on the wall.

How best to begin? Well, *don't* sit down and rush through the book as if you were reading a bestseller! Finish this introduction and read the next section which gives valuable information about tools and materials. Then browse through the book, look at the pictures and select the game that looks most attractive to you. Read how to make it and decide whether it is a game you want to make for yourself, or give to a friend.

The games described in this book range from those that have been around for centuries to others that are newly invented. Some of the more complex games take time to construct and a good assortment of woodworking tools will be useful. But you can make other games quickly out of paper, using buttons or coins or checkers for playing pieces.

Before You Begin

Tools and Materials

You need only a few basic tools to build most of the games in this book. You'll need at least the following items for a start:

a mitre box with a fine-toothed saw
one or two medium-size C-clamps
a utility knife with changeable blades
a metal straightedge
a hand drill
a measuring stick
a hammer
a rasp
an assortment of sandpaper

These are basic tools that you probably have around the house. When you need to bore holes, an electric hand drill simplifies the job tremendously. If you enjoy working with wood, you can hardly do without one.

If you decide to construct more than one game from this book (perhaps to give as gifts), keep a small supply of materials on hand. Next weekend may be completely ruined by rain and you can build a game that will keep the whole family busy and entertained. You'll need:

at least 5 colors of paint for wood
clear lacquer (not necessary if you use paint that dries to a
    glossy or semi-glossy finish, also available in spray cans)
a few bristle and watercolor brushes
cellulose tape
white liquid glue
wood primer
clear wood finish
a small supply of plywood, molding and dowels

Which Finish for Which Material?

It seems as if an infinite number of finishes are available to the hobbyist and it is often difficult to tell the difference between them. The important thing to know is which materials to use them on (metal, plastic, wood, and so forth), something you can learn by reading the labels. It is particularly important to study this when you work with plastic, because many finishes will corrode the material. Your local supplier can give you advice on available finishes.

Drills

Many of the games in this book are "peg" games—the playing "men" are in the form of dowel pins which fit into holes bored in the game board.

You can purchase dowel in 3-ft. (or 1-metre) lengths and in diameters of $\frac{1}{4}$, $\frac{5}{16}$, $\frac{3}{8}$, $\frac{1}{2}$, $\frac{5}{8}$, $\frac{3}{4}$ and 1 inch (8, 10, 12, 14 mm. in metric measure), made of hardwood. Spiral twist bits are available in sizes at intervals of $\frac{1}{16}$ inch (0.5 mm.) up to $\frac{3}{8}$ inch (10 mm.). Larger size twist bits are expensive, but the flat type bit shown in Illus. 1 is quite reasonable. They are available in increments of $\frac{1}{8}$ inch (2 mm.).

A problem arises in fitting dowels into the bored holes, because a $\frac{5}{8}$-inch dowel, for instance, won't slide easily into a $\frac{5}{8}$-inch hole, yet fits too loosely in a hole $\frac{3}{4}$ inch in diameter. To solve this problem, buy a $\frac{5}{8}$-inch flat wood bit and bore a sample

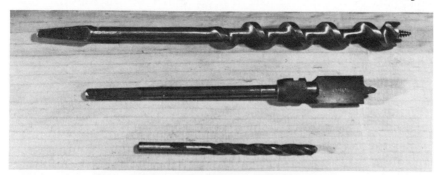

Illus. 1. The wide variety of drill bits available allows you to make holes of almost any size.

Illus. 2. Be sure that dowels fit snugly into the holes you drill, but not so tightly they cannot be lifted out easily.

hole in a scrap board. Test a piece of $\frac{5}{8}$-inch dowel to see if perhaps it fits. Sometimes a flat drill cuts a little larger than its marked size, so the hole will be an easy fit for the dowel (even when it is painted!). If this happens, the whole affair is simple, and in peg games you can use basically $\frac{5}{8}$-inch (16-mm.) dowels.

If the test boring shows that the hole is just a little too tight for an easy fit, move the drill around in a circle, reaming while boring the hole and this will widen it slightly. If the hole is really too tight and this manoeuvre does not work, you have the alternative of sanding the dowels down or buying the next larger size of flat drill bit to grind (or file) it down until it bores a hole just slightly larger than the dowel. Whether you use a file or a grinding wheel, keep the amount of reduction the same on both sides so that the point remains centered, and keep checking as you work by boring test holes and trying the dowel.

How to Treat Wood Surfaces

If you want to keep the natural color and grain of the wood and, at the same time, protect it from damage, do not use a lacquer but a sealer and paste wood filler. First, sand the wood surface smooth with fine-grained sandpaper. Apply the sealer with a brush. It soaks into the pores of the wood—and the surface is dry in 10 minutes. Any little specks of wood left over from the sanding will make the surface of the wood feel slightly rough, so it has to be lightly sanded again.

Next, take a piece of soft cloth (an old undershirt or something of the kind) and fold it over until you have a firm, fist-sized handful that is half-rounded like a ball. Slightly dampen the pad with the paste wood filler and lay down a light coating over the surface of the wood. Rub the wood lightly in the direction of the grain, laying one stroke next to the preceding one. Repeat the procedure a second time and allow the work to dry. This gives the wood a very light, fine, satin finish. The wood surface now has a pleasant feel to it and is protected against moisture, and spotting.

Color Finish for Wood

If you want to apply a coat of matt color finish to wood, you can use any of the readily available brands of house paint. You can also use show-card colors, but these generally will not withstand hard use. Many color finishes for wood have a water base which means that they can be thinned as needed with water; also the brushes can be washed out with water (as long as the paint has not dried in the bristles!).

This paint dries to a matt finish which can be given an attractive, fine-satin look by brushing it vigorously with a clothes brush. You can also paint over the color surface with clear lacquer to give the object a more or less glossy finish, depending on the type of lacquer.

If you want to color wood but still retain its natural grain, use wood stain instead of paint.

Games that may be subjected to rough handling or repeated use should be finished with a tough acrylic lacquer. This, however, may depend on circumstances, since lacquer takes some time to dry. You can also use car finish lacquer which is available in spray cans. It is somewhat more expensive, but it dries very quickly and is available in attractive colors, including metallic finishes, which are very elegant for games!

For small projects you can use tubes of artist's acrylic paint. The colors are brighter and they dry to a matt or glossy surface depending upon the medium you use to thin them.

Stains

When you want to retain the grain of the wood, but change its color, use a stain. Wood stains are available, ready for use, in small cans. There are oil-base stains and the more modern, faster drying, acrylic-base stains. Spread the stain on the raw, sanded wood with a brush. Repeated applications deepen the intensity of the color. After drying (2-3 hours), sand lightly and apply a primer. Again sand lightly and apply paste wood filler.

If you want to give the wood surface particular resistance to damage or produce a glossy surface, apply a coat of clear lacquer over the primer.

Keep in mind, however, that a high gloss surface also scratches quickly and no longer looks so beautiful. You can fill in scratches on matt-finished wood by simply going over the surface lightly with paste wood filler.

Cutting Lengths of Molding or Strips of Thin Wood

In many of the games, molding or wood strips must be cut into pieces of equal length to be used as playing pieces. It is a nuisance to have to measure off the same length each time before you saw. There is a way to avoid this. First, clamp your mitre box to the worktable with a C-clamp. Then, at the proper distance from the saw blade, clamp a "stop block"—a small piece of wood—to the bed of the mitre box. After each cut, remove the sawed-off section and push the remaining strip up against the stop. By repeating the procedure, you will be able to cut all of the pieces to exactly the same length.

Illus. 3. Use a mitre box to assure square cuts. A "stop block" clamped inside the box will enable you to cut off multiple pieces of the same length without measuring and marking for each cut.

Where to Buy Material?

Lumber and paint supply stores can be found in every city. Sometimes you can find wood remnants and short lengths of molding or strip material in the "grab box" at a hobby shop or lumberyard where wood is cut to order. Keep your eyes open as you shop, as some interesting piece of molding or an unusual material may give you an idea for a future project.

Games for One

The first group of projects is devoted to games that you play alone or one player at a time. On-lookers can join in the fun too and, of course, several people can play at the same time if you construct more than one set!

Not only are these games pleasant pastimes, but they also exercise your powers of concentration, sharpen your wits, and develop skill and a steady hand—not only in playing them, but in making them as well. These games will cheer you up when you are lonesome, amuse you when you have to wait and relax you after a day of hard work. Games for single players serve very well to entertain the early arrivals for an evening of competitive group games and to occupy any players who are "out" of other games.

Illus. 4. This is how the Magic Cube looks when it is properly assembled.

THE MAGIC CUBE

For the Puzzle Fiend

Even an expert may end up gnashing his teeth over this puzzle! You can entertain an entire group with it—everyone wants to try it once (and thinks he can solve it faster!). Simple to make, it is a challenging and rewarding game.

HOW TO PLAY

(*Playing Time:* 5 minutes and up)

A large checkerboard-pattern cube is enclosed in a wooden box. Tip the box and the cube falls out into pieces. The object now is to reassemble the cube so that it fits into the box. Of course, it must show the correct checkerboard pattern on all sides. Look simple? Try it!

HOW TO BUILD

The basic cubes can be readily cut from a length of square pine molding. "Baluster" is the thing to ask for at your lumber supply dealer and the standard $\frac{3}{4} \times \frac{3}{4}$-inch $(2 \times 2$-cm.) or $1\frac{1}{8} \times 1\frac{1}{8}$-inch (about 3×3-cm.) size is about right for this game. In calculating how long a piece of molding you will need for 27 cubes, be sure to allow a few extra inches to make up for the material the saw cuts away (the "kerf"). The important thing is to cut the cubes so they are exactly square. Clamp a stop in your mitre box to assure that all the cubes will be alike. Cut one cube first, sand the two rough ends as much as you plan to, check the dimensions of the piece and adjust the stop, if necessary, before cutting the rest of the cubes

Paint 14 cubes one color, 13 cubes another color. Use glossy-finish paint or coat with clear lacquer.

Assemble the large cube by taking groups of 2 to 5 of the smaller cubes and glueing them together in their assembled position, so that you end up with 5 to 8 single pieces. You will find that when you glue the cubes together into three-dimensional shapes, the puzzle is more difficult to reassemble.

Illus. 5. The large cube is made up of 27 smaller cubes, some of which are glued together.

When glueing, work carefully and reassemble the ultimate cube repeatedly to check it. It's also a good idea to make yourself some notes or at least to mark a corner to serve as a starting place, as otherwise you may find that you yourself are not able to solve the puzzle!

The construction of the "packaging" or box for the puzzle is clear from the illustration. The basic material is $\frac{1}{4}$- or $\frac{3}{8}$-inch (about 1-cm.) plywood, hardboard or pine slats from old orange crates. Since the outer dimensions of the large cube tend to "grow" as you add layers of paint and glue between the individual pieces, it is better to put off making the box until the puzzle itself is completed. Even then you should make the inside dimension of the box at least $\frac{1}{8}$ inch (3 mm.) larger than the big cube so that it can be inserted and tipped out easily.

Assemble the box using brads and glue to hold the pieces together. Sandpaper the inside and outside, the edges and corners, and paint to match or contrast with the cubes.

Variations

This game looks quite elegant if the cubes are made from wood of contrasting colors, such as pine and mahogany, and given a clear finish. This is a job for a dedicated and precise craftsman, but the end product is especially decorative.

You can often find strips and sheets of various woods in a wide variety of sizes in model-builder's supply stores or their catalogues if your lumberyard can't supply you. After cutting, you should carefully sand the cubes with very fine sandpaper, and assemble the individual parts with glue. Finally, treat the surfaces with sealer and paste wood filler before varnishing. In this way, you make the most out of the natural beauty of the wood.

Illus. 6. An attractive variation is to use a clear finish which enhances the natural grain of the wood.

THE ENDLESS STRIPE

Taxes Your Brain and Your Patience

This block of 8 single cubes is not only a challenge to assemble, it is also a small, attractive room decoration which can be changed around time and again into different patterns. It is easy to make, though painting the stripe requires a certain amount of precision. If you give up quickly, don't try this game!

HOW TO PLAY
(*Playing time:* 10 minutes and up)

The 8 cubes must be set together into a block so that the multi-colored stripe that appears at least once on each face of the small cubes is connected into a continuous ribbon running all around the outside of the block.

Since the surfaces of the small cubes that lie out of sight inside the large block also carry a stripe design, proper assembly is a devilish task.

Luckily, the game is so pretty that once you begin it, you can leave it sitting on the table until you work out the solution, without its looking like something that should have been cleared away.

HOW TO BUILD

Start by making 8 identical wooden cubes about $1\frac{1}{2}$ inches (approximately 4 cm.) square. Paint the wooden cubes all the same base color. Assemble them into a block (held together with rubber bands), and sketch the stripe with a pencil. A ruler and a French curve may be useful for drawing the stripe.

The game is more difficult if you don't just run the stripe from one cube-face to another, but draw it across one face and later bring it back to cross that face again. You may be able to create a more harmonious, decorative design by planning it out on paper first as in Illus. 8.

Using 3 or 4 different colors and a very fine watercolor brush, paint on the stripes. If necessary, make a guide strip of card-

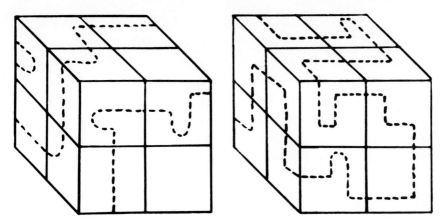

Illus. 7. Plan your stripe before starting to paint.

board and run the brush along its edge for a smooth line. Don't worry about your hand shaking a little; slightly "jittery" lines make the whole thing even more appealing. Just be sure that the stripes meet exactly where they connect from block to block!

Now take the cubes apart and paint their inside faces in the same style so that the players will mistake them for stripes.

Illus. 8. Here is a partially assembled puzzle. Make a storage box of wood or sheet plastic.

You may find it helpful to paint a closed circle on the inner sides as an aid toward solving the puzzle. When the two circles are laid together, one upon the other, the cube is correctly assembled.

Brush the finished cubes with a clothes brush to give them a soft, satin finish. For storage, choose a ready-made box, or saw the sides for one out of wood or sheet plastic and glue them together with the proper adhesive.

Variations

For a really beautiful game, try making this one out of *big* blocks. Cubes left in their natural wood color also look attractive with colorful stripes painted on them. For a pocket game, make small cubes and draw the stripe patterns with a felt-tip pen. You can carry the game in your pocket and use it to while away waiting periods, and it makes a fine gift for friends who like intricate puzzles.

Illus. 9. The goal of the 3-D Puzzle is to construct a large cube with the component blocks of each face showing the same design. A wooden tray that you can build easily serves to store the game and makes an attractive display in itself.

THE 3–D PUZZLE CUBE
A Puzzle in Three Dimensions

Illus. 10. The yellow-edged cube serves as a pattern to show you which symbol each side should display.

You need a great deal of concentration and patience to work out the solution to this game. Don't give it to people who are particularly nervous—or maybe you should!

The hard part is to construct a cube so that each side shows the same symbol in the same colors. This is made more difficult by the fact that each symbol is used in positive and negative form and, moreover, in similar colors.

When you aren't playing with the game, you can hang it on the wall in an open box. It is an eye-catching "picture" that can be changed simply by turning the cubes to show new and different combinations of color and shape. You can also leave it out on a table as a kind of free-form construction.

Children especially enjoy this game and often work it out with astonishing speed. Try it with the whole family—it goes quicker that way and everybody has fun!

HOW TO PLAY
(*Playing time:* 30 minutes and up)

The object is to construct a single cube out of 27 smaller ones so that each side of the large cube shows only one design of the same color. A 28th, yellow-edged cube serves as the pattern to show which symbol each side should carry. Illus. 10 shows a partially assembled cube with one side already completed.

Variations

You can invent other ways of playing, too, so that each face shows a particular pattern.

HOW TO BUILD

Cut 28 identical wooden blocks about 1½ inch (4 cm.) square. Paint all of the cubes the same base color. When they are dry, assemble them into one large cube. Using cut-out patterns of thin cardboard, draw the outlines of circles, squares, or whatever designs you choose onto the cube faces with a sharp pencil. Paint them in with a fine brush (the better the brush, the easier it will be to fill in the outlines accurately). Then take apart the big cube and paint designs on the remaining blank faces so that each cube has six different faces.

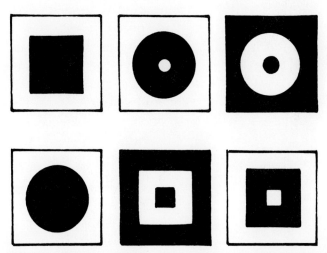

Illus. 11. You can use any designs you want on your blocks so long as you have six different ones. The game is more interesting if you use the same symbols but reverse the colors for another face.

Making the Box

Make the outside frame from a strip of 1×2-inch (actual measure $\frac{3}{4} \times 1\frac{1}{2}$-inch—about 2-cm. $\times$ 4-cm.) lumber. Be sure to cut it at least $\frac{1}{8}$ inch (3 mm.) wider and longer inside than your blocks measure when they are laid flat. Cut the bottom of the box from $\frac{1}{4}$-inch plywood or some similar material and glue or nail the parts together. Paint the box to match the background color of the blocks. Finally, apply furniture wax to all the parts and buff them with a soft brush. This will keep the color finish from collecting fingerprints and will give it a light sheen.

Turn two screw eyes into the back side of one of the long sides of the frame and use them to hang the box and its contents on a wall.

THE TURNCOATS
Relax with these "Pin-Head" Pegs

Illus. 12.

In politics, a person who changes sides is called a "turncoat." In these games, two parties change sides in the fewest possible moves. Several variations of the game are possible.

Both of the games described here can be played in a short time. Even so, you will have to use your head a little and give the games a few tries before you find the solutions. Changing sides is not as simple as it seems.

These games, in attractively grained wood, make ideal gifts. If you have an electric drill to use, you should be able to construct them within a half hour.

HOW TO PLAY

(Playing time: 10 minutes and up)

Game 1

This game is played on a board with 7 holes in it. Three pegs of one color stand at one end of the board, 3 pegs of a different color at the other end. The goal is to have the two sets of pegs change places. A peg can either move forward one hole when the hole ahead is open or jump over another peg when the hole beyond it is unoccupied. The figures can only move forward, never backwards. Complete the switch within 15 moves. (For the solution, see p. 79.)

Game 2

This game features 4 pegs on each side and it follows the same rules as Game 1, except that the pegs must change places within 24 moves. To help you keep track of the moves, mark the individual holes with letters of the alphabet. (Solution on p. 79.)

HOW TO BUILD

The game board itself is made from a $\frac{3}{4}$-inch thick (2-cm.) strip of hardwood such as mahogany, cut about 10 inches (25 cm.) long by $2\frac{1}{2}$ inches (6 cm.) wide. Clean and smooth the strip with sandpaper. Drill 7 or 9 holes (depending on which game you want to make) equal distances apart making them slightly wider than the diameter of the pegs. To ensure that you drill all of the holes to the same depth, wrap a piece of colored tape around the bit to serve as a depth-gauge. Drill each hole about $\frac{5}{8}$ inch (15 mm.) deep.

Make the pegs from a $\frac{5}{8}$-inch (16-mm.) diameter dowel (6 or 8 pieces, depending on the game) each about $2\frac{3}{8}$ inches (6 cm.) long. Using a mitre box, cut pieces $2\frac{1}{2}$ inches (about 6 cm.) long. Glue wooden balls which you can buy ready-made at a hobby supply store, to the ends of the pegs. To color the wood while still retaining its natural grain, use wood stain instead of paint. When the stain is dry, rub some wax on the pegs and board and polish them lightly.

Variations

Illus. 12 shows the 8-peg game with the holes drilled into the bottom of a box. The piece at the bottom is a sliding cover. The pegs tuck away into the box when no one is playing the game. The box has two small playing surfaces for other games painted on the sides. This project is for a somewhat more experienced home craftsman.

THE CHESS KNIGHT GAME
For Sharp Thinkers

A solitaire game that was played a great deal during the 19th century, this requires deep thought, patience and concentration. Chess players especially can have a lot of fun with it.

The Knight Game is similar to the Turncoat game—but more playing men are involved and they move differently; namely, like the knights in chess (see How to Play).

The red knights must change places with the blue ones in the fewest possible number of steps, moving as the knights move in chess. Don't think that this is child's play! The first time you try it, you will probably get several knights so hopelessly walled in that you will feel like smashing the game! To finish in 50 moves is a respectable showing.

If you build this game with love and care, it will be so pretty that you can hang it on the wall.

HOW TO PLAY

(Playing time: 20 minutes and up)

Set 12 red and 12 blue knights in place on the game board, as shown in Illus. 14. Leave the middle square empty. The knights move diagonally—either one square forward and two sideways, or two forward and one sideways—in any direction. Illus. 13 shows this clearly.

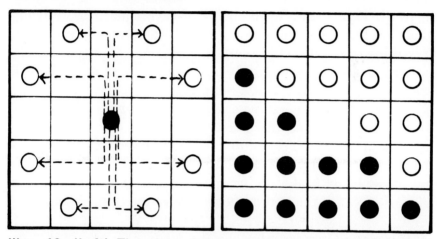

Illus. 13. (Left) The chess knight piece can move one square forwards or backwards, then two squares to left or right; or it can go two squares forwards or backwards, then one square to left or right. (Right) Starting position for the two sides.

Your goal is to bring the playing men back into the same relative position on the opposite side of the board in the fewest possible moves. While you should finish the game within 50 moves, it is almost impossible to do it in less than 45.

Try other starting positions. You can vary them as much as you like, but your goal is always the same.

HOW TO BUILD

Making the Board

To simplify drilling holes to a uniform depth, make the bottom of the game board from two pieces of wood. Drill all the way through one of the boards and then attach it to the other which will act as a "stop." Make the peg board from a 12-inch (30-cm.) square of $\frac{3}{8}$- or $\frac{1}{2}$-inch (10- to 15-mm.) slab of plywood. Cover the board with a primer coat of paint. First marking off a border equal to the thickness of the wood you plan to use as a frame, divide the remaining surface area into 25 equal-size squares. You can paint the squares the same colors as the playing men; or you can outline them as in Illus. 14. The center square, which remains empty, is specially marked. Determine the midpoint of each square by drawing diagonal lines and drill a hole through the center of each one. For this game you should use $\frac{1}{4}$-inch (6-mm.) diameter dowels, so use a drill bit that is slightly larger or else plan to sand down the ends of the dowel. Test a piece of the dowel you plan to use for the knights to see if it fits easily into the holes. Paint colorful border circles around the holes.

Glue the second piece of material for the bottom which can be thinner plywood or even hardboard under the board with the holes in it. Make the frame from a thin wood strip and glue or nail it to the bottom board. Paint the frame black.

Making the Gamesmen

For the tops of the gamesmen, you can use ready-made wooden balls or rounded wooden drawer pulls. Bore them with the drill so that you can fit in the ends of the dowel pins. Then cut 24 pieces of dowel each $1\frac{1}{4}$ inches (3 cm.) long, and glue them into the wood balls. Paint 12 of the playing men red, the other 12 blue.

As a final touch, apply a coat of clear brushing lacquer to both the playing board and the men.

Variations

You can, of course, play this game without going to the trouble of constructing pegs and an elaborate board. Use any wooden playing board painted with the appropriate squares and 12 each of two colors of tiddlywinks. If you need more playing boards in a hurry—if you decide to have a tournament, for example—simply draw the game board pattern on paper and play with buttons, tiddlywinks, or coins.

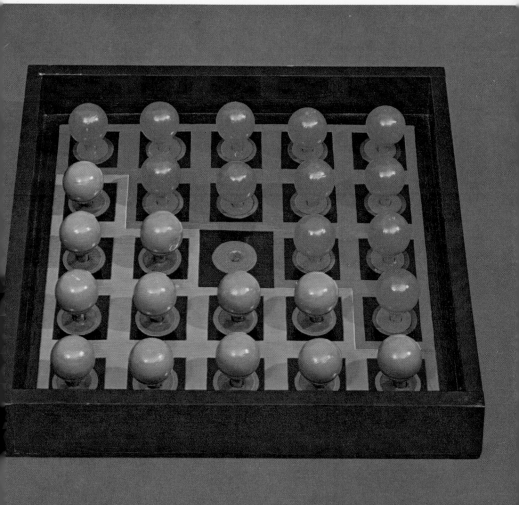

Illus. 14. This set of gamesmen was made by fitting ready-made wooden balls onto wooden dowels. Other possibilities are easy to think up though—many different shapes of wooden drawer pulls, for example, are available.

THE LABYRINTH
It's Attractive on the Wall Too

As the angle of light in your room shifts with the time of day, the labyrinth hanging on a wall also presents an ever-changing pattern. It is easy to build and gives you the opportunity to construct cunning traps, obstacles and slip-through passageways that are fun to devise.

HOW TO PLAY
(Playing time: about 5 minutes)

The object is to move the ball bearing from the center of the spiral at one side of the board to the center of the spiral on the opposite side of the board. Study the layout of the board carefully before you start, and you should be able to get through on your first try. The winner is the one who gets the ball through the maze in the shortest period of time.

HOW TO BUILD

Making the Box

You can use a large, flat ready-made box or construct one yourself. Paint the box a single color on the bottom and around the sides. Cut a supply of strips the same width as the box sides from a piece of poster board. You can curl the cardboard strips where necessary by pulling them down over the edge of a table. Begin with the locations Start and Goal, glueing the spiral strips in place. Next lay out a route for the ball to follow. Make the path as intricate as possible with many turns and twists. Place cardboard strips loosely along the route, then cut little openings and passages in some of the strips, and create a few covered or hidden tunnels. Fill in the remaining areas of the board with false paths and dead-end traps.

Paint the whole board here and there, with differently colored felt-tip pens, and be as misleading as possible, of course, so that the player will run into nothing but trouble in finding the right way through.

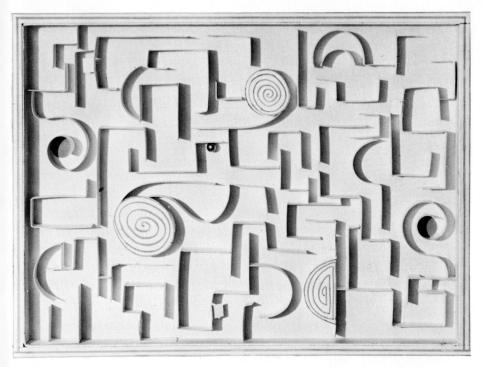

Illus. 15. The object of this game is to work the ball from the dark circle at one side of the board to the dark circle at the opposite side. Use your ingenuity to lay out a board with plenty of dead-end traps and false paths to make the labyrinth a real challenge for the players.

If the cardboard box does not seem to be stiff enough, you can glue a framework of thin wood strips around the sides and glue the bottom of the box to a piece of plywood. A thin piece of sheet plastic over the top will protect the labyrinth from dust.

Variations

A labyrinth of color patterns, made of differently colored cardboard strips, is very pretty and fun to build. Your reward is a "picture" to hang on the wall and a game you can play!

THE DON'T BE NERVOUS GAME
Not for Impatient People

Here at last is a game which doesn't require much thought to play. Though your head is spared, your nerves are not! This game should not be inflicted on people who are under stress and strain: never take it to the office with you.

HOW TO PLAY
(*Playing time:* 3 minutes and up)

This is where you have to be ve-e-ery calm. Don't jiggle or you'll never succeed in rolling the 4 steel balls each into the middle circle of one of the groups of concentric circles. The fatal hurdle is that the entrances to the various groups are located exactly opposite each other! When you get two of the steel balls "inside," they tend to slip right out again as you tilt the board to roll the third in! This really calls for concentration and steady hands. Some people never succeed at this game, while others can do it only when they are relaxed.

HOW TO BUILD
Making the Box

Start with a ready-made square box or make one from a piece of thin wood and some framing lumber. It is important that the bottom of the game board be absolutely level and smooth, so that the steel balls will roll uniformly and easily. Sandpaper the wood smooth and paint the box inside and out with show-card colors. Cut strips of thin cardboard and paint stripes on them with felt-tipped pens. Carefully pull the strips over the edge of a table to curve them and cut them into lengths to make up the 4 triple circles. Cut one or two small entryways into each circle. Glue the cardboard circles to the bottom of the box.

Steel ball bearings work best for this game but you can substitute glass marbles if necessary. You may want to attach a piece of glass or sheet plastic to the top of the box.

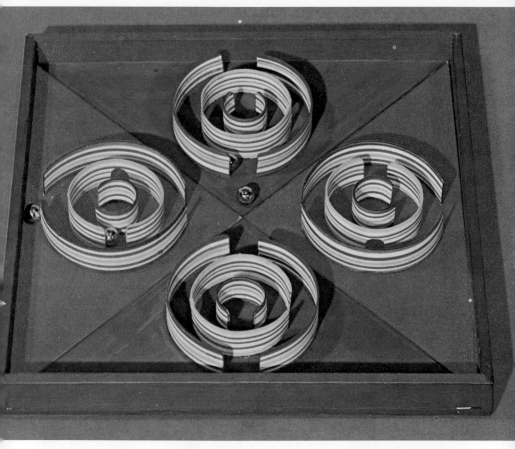

Illus. 16. With this game, gravity often sends the balls rolling again just as you near success. These colorful board games make attractive decorations even when they are not in use.

SOLITAIRE
Old, but Truly Fascinating

The age and origin of solitaire, also called "the hermit's game" and "the priest's game," are shrouded in darkness. The monks of the Middle Ages are said to have played it a great deal, and the Spanish conquistadors reported that the Indians played it with arrows stuck in the ground.

Illus. 17. This is the starting position for the game of Solitaire.

HOW TO PLAY
(*Playing time:* about 15 minutes and up)

The classic field of play is cross-shaped, with 33 positions. At the start, gamesmen (ball bearings or marbles) occupy all the positions except the middle one. The only move allowed is a jump, one man over another, so long as the position beyond is unoccupied. The man jumped is removed from the board. You can only jump vertically or horizontally, never diagonally.

The object of the game is to remove all the playing pieces from the board, until only one, the "solitaire"—which cannot jump over and remove itself—is left. To make the game more difficult, the last ball on the last move of the game must occupy the center position. That is not as easy to accomplish as it may seem! You can be pleased with yourself if you succeed in

			㉛	㉜	㉝			
			㉘	㉙	㉚			
㉑	㉒	㉓	㉔	㉕	㉖	㉗
⑭	⑮	⑯	17	⑱	⑲	⑳
⑦	⑧	⑨	⑩	⑪	⑫	⑬
			④	⑤	⑥			
			①	②	③			

Illus. 18. Use this number sequence to follow the solution given on page 79—or to record your own moves.

finishing up with only one piece (not two or three), anywhere on the board. If you give up, use the number sequence in Illus. 18 to follow the moves given on p. 79.

After you have gained some experience with the game, try to clear the pieces away so that the remaining ones are arranged as in Illus. 19 (the solutions are given on p. 79).

HOW TO BUILD

Making the Board

First saw the plywood board to size and smooth the edges. Cutting a circle is hard work without a power saw, but you can

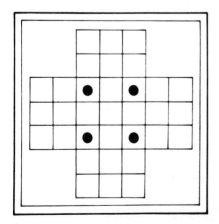
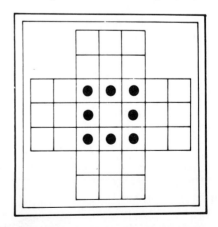

Illus. 19. The goal of this game is to end up with the remaining pieces in a predetermined arrangement such as these two examples.

use a square board just as well. Divide the board into squares which represent the playing field. Find the center-point of each square and mark it as a drilling point. Bore the holes about ⅜ inch (1 cm.) deep, and to keep them uniformly at the right depth, mark the shank of the drill with a piece of colored tape. Smooth the surface with sandpaper. Apply stain if you wish to change the color of the wood; use a sealer and paste wood filler if you prefer to preserve the natural color and grain. Put ball bearings or marbles in the holes and you're ready to play.

Variations

Instead of round balls, you can saw off short lengths of dowel and use them as pegs. Any wood with an attractive grain, such as pine, will do.

You can also change the pattern of the holes in the game board to add pieces, making the game more difficult. A 35-move solution is given on p. 79.

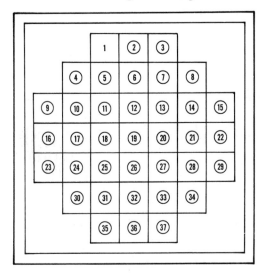

Illus. 20. You can make this game more difficult by using a 37-hole board.

Illus. 21. (Opposite page) This attractive kit can be used for a number of different games. Here, the board is set up in the starting position for Salta. See page 41.

Games for Two

It is a great satisfaction to play with games you have designed yourself and built with your own hands. It is even more fun when two can play.

Like most of the games in this book, those in this chapter are mental games; you need skill and foresight to plan your tactics. Sometimes the solution takes quite a while, other times it comes quickly. When two people play, you not only have to plan and carry out your own moves, you also have to be able to see through the plans of your opponent and, if possible, thwart them or turn them to your own advantage. But winning the game, outwitting an opponent, or developing a tactic, is only part of the fun. The best part is the delight you get in the thorough exercise of your reasoning ability. You will feel

marvelously relaxed when you have played an exciting game you really had to break your head over! Generally, you put your mind into gear only when "serious things" with important consequences are involved. How satisfying it is to think simply to enjoy it!

GAME KIT

Five Games for Good Strategists

Here is a boxful of games for two players ranging from the comparatively "fast" Reversi which takes about 30 minutes, to the game of Conquest which may go on for several hours. The cover of the box has a game board on both sides.

HOW TO BUILD

Making the Box

Cut two 14-inch (35-cm.) square pieces of $\frac{1}{4}$-inch (6-mm.) plywood for the top and bottom of the box. Make the sides of the box from $\frac{1}{4} \times \frac{7}{8}$-inch (about 6×22-mm.) strips of wood. You can buy these as ready-made moldings called "lattice." Glue the strips to the bottom piece of plywood to form a frame. Glue in additional strips to divide the interior. Use strips $\frac{1}{4} \times \frac{1}{2}$ inch (about 6×13 mm.) to make the frame for the cover. You may have to cut down a piece of lattice, but these dimensions are only suggestions and can be altered to suit available material.

Paint the box red, except for the cover, where you need to paint only the inside and outside edges. Divide the inner face of the cover into a field of 9×9 squares, the outer face into a field of 10×10 squares. Use a ruler, marking lightly with a lead pencil. Cut squares of the proper size out of black and silver colored paper. When the fit is right, glue them down. Outline the 9 squares in the center of the 9×9 board by painting or glueing down red strips.

Lay the cover on the box, flat side down. This will keep the playing pieces in their own compartments. Attach small clasps to two opposite sides to hold the top and bottom of the box together.

Making the Playing Pieces

You will need a variety of playing pieces for the different games. For Reversi, you will need 100 round pieces that are white on one side, red on the other. You can glue plastic tiddlywinks together or start with white ones only, painting one side with red nail polish.

Warfare requires 30 playing pieces—15 red and 15 white. Use ordinary tiddlywinks or saw pieces off the end of a length of dowel.

For Conquest, you will need 18 "men" that you can saw from a length of $\frac{5}{8}$-inch (16-mm.) dowel. Make each piece $1\frac{1}{2}$ inches tall (about 4 cm.) and use a mitre box to ensure that the ends are flat. Otherwise the playing pieces will not stand up straight. Paint 9 of them red, the other 9 blue and mark one piece of each color to designate it as "King." (Paint the end surfaces a different color or put stripes around it.)

Salta calls for 30 wooden squares, half of them blue, the other half red, with each piece marked with a number from 1 to 15. You can buy rub-on numbers at art supply stores. The pieces themselves can be sawed off the end of a piece of $\frac{3}{4}$-inch (2-cm.) square molding.

For Little Boxes you will need a number of thin strips of wood cut into pieces of equal length, so that 4 pieces can be laid neatly around a square. Paint them red. You can use 200 pieces, but 100 will do, if you want to play a shorter game. Make these "fence" pieces from a strip of small molding such as "glass bead" or you can use pieces of wooden matches.

Finally, write the rules of the game in a small notebook, and place it in the box with the playing pieces.

Variation

Make the Conquest board in small, portable size with holes and pegs as playing pieces.

HOW TO PLAY

Reversi

(*Playing time:* 30 minutes and up)

This is a brief, exciting game that your grandparents liked to play.

You play this game on the board with 10 squares across. The playing men are flat, round pieces—red on one side, white on the other—and each player starts out with 50 pieces. All the game squares are used, both black and silver squares. Alternating turns, each player puts down one piece at a time. One player places his men red side up, the other player white side up.

The goal is to block or "enclose" your enemy's pieces in horizontal, vertical or diagonal lines with two of your own pieces, one at each end of the line in question. The enclosed pieces are turned over so that they show the same color as the two blocking pieces. This does not prevent a player from trying to enclose this line again with his own men and so win back the lost pieces.

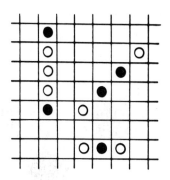

Illus. 22. The goal of Reversi is to enclose your opponent's pieces in vertical, diagonal or horizontal lines as in these examples.

The game ends when all the playing pieces have been set down. You will find that a wild hassle soon develops around the corner positions.

Even though playing one piece may enclose more than one line, you can turn over only one row of enemy pieces in a turn. Enclosures made after the pieces are turned over, naturally, do not count.

A variation of this game is to start with 4 playing pieces placed in the middle of the board. From the fifth piece on, each player has to place a piece so as to enclose and turn over an enemy. If he cannot, he must skip his turn until a possibility presents itself. This is a matter of horizontal and vertical lines. The winner is the player who, after the last play, has the greatest number of pieces of his own color showing on the board.

Conquest
(*Playing time:* 30 minutes and up)

An exciting game for sharp minds capable of concentration. It looks harmless but is really exciting!

Use the playing board with 9 large squares across. Each player has 9 pieces, one of them specially marked as "King." You start with the playing pieces set up in clusters in diagonally opposite corners, using both black and white squares as shown in Illus. 23. The object of both sides is to take possession of the "fortress"—the large square outlined in red in the middle of

Illus. 23. Conquest calls for a board with a large middle area marked off as a "fortress" and two playing pieces specially marked as "Kings."

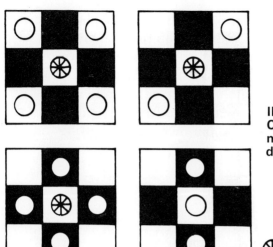

Illus. 24. A player wins at Conquest by moving his men into certain pre-determined positions as in these examples.

 = King

the board. This is accomplished by moving your men into positions agreed upon before the game begins (see Illus. 24).

The most important rule is that each playing piece can move only on squares of the same color it was on at the start of the game. In effect, this means that pieces move only diagonally but they can go in any of the four possible directions. Players take turns with the beginner chosen by lot. No piece can be jumped, not your own nor your opponent's.

Your opponent's men are eliminated by enclosing or surrounding them (see Illus. 25). An "enclosure" is valid only if all the pieces involved are on squares of the same color. Horizontal or vertical enclosures are, therefore, impossible. Enclosed pieces are not removed from the board, but sent into "exile." The enclosing player can place the piece on any unoccupied square he wishes, usually, of course, as far as possible from the fortress. You can enclose several pieces at the same time—but be careful—you may be trapped in an enclosure yourself without expecting it! Then your enemy will banish your men in the same manner.

You have to play this game a few times before you recognize its many tactical possibilities!

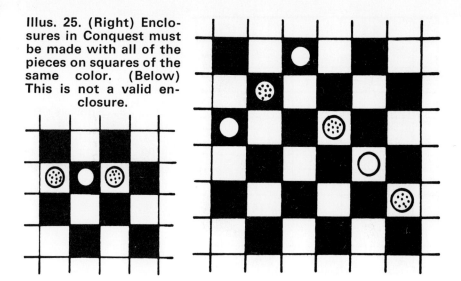

Illus. 25. (Right) Enclosures in Conquest must be made with all of the pieces on squares of the same color. (Below) This is not a valid enclosure.

Salta

(*Playing time:* 60 minutes and up)

This is a "place-changing" game that was invented by a musician during the last century. The name Salta is derived from the Latin word "saltare"—to jump. The game quickly attracted many fans and even "Salta Societies" sprang up. Today, Salta has been somewhat forgotten although it is really fun to play.

The original game consists of a board with 100 squares and 15 playing pieces for each player, each set a different color. The pieces were originally marked in groups of 5 with the sun, moon, and stars. To simplify them for our game, number each set from 1 to 15. (See page 35.)

Both players lay out their pieces with the numbers 1–15 in the order shown in Illus. 26, using only the black squares. Your goal is to change places with the opposing pieces—at the end of the game, your pieces should stand in the exact same places as your opponent's did at the start. Blue piece #1 should stand where red piece #1 is in the picture—diagonally opposite its starting place.

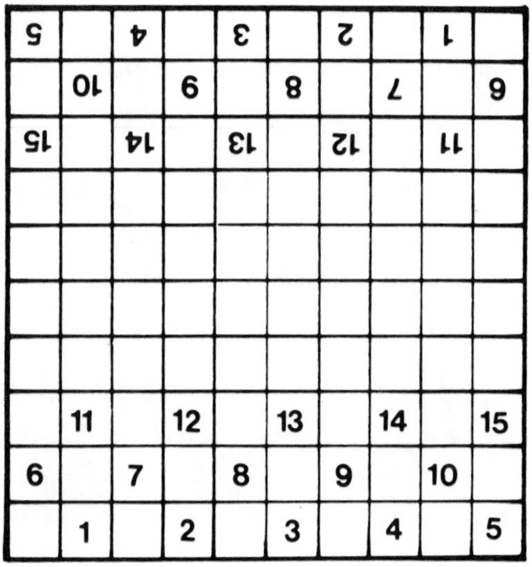

5		4		3		2		1	
	10		9		8		7		6
15		14		13		12		11	
	11		12		13		14		15
6		7		8		9		10	
	1		2		3		4		5

Illus. 26. This is the starting position for Salta, with the numbered playing pieces arranged in order on the dark squares.

Each piece can move diagonally forward or backward, one square at a time. You are allowed to jump only when you're moving forward and you can jump over only one piece at a time, so long as the square beyond it is empty. In this game, when you have an opportunity to jump, you must take it. Part of your strategy then is to try to force your opponent's men to jump—in the wrong direction, of course! If you have several opportunities to jump, you are allowed to make only one of them. Red always begins the game, and blue has the last play. The winner is the first player to get his pieces into correct position.

One more rule of the game is that if neither player has all of his men in position by the 120th move, you stop playing and calculate how many moves each player would have to make to get all of his men in position using the shortest possible route. The player who would require the least number of moves is declared the winner.

As you approach the final moves, a good player tries to block his opponent, forcing him far out of his way. That way, at the reckoning after the 120th move, the opponent will have a farther way to go and, consequently, loses the game. The trick in Salta is to remain in control of the general direction of your own pieces in spite of your opponent's attempts to force them aside. A couple of thoughtless moves can set you back considerably in this game.

Salta is especially good for players who enjoy long battles and involved tactics.

Warfare
(*Playing time:* 30 minutes and up)

Developed from the Chinese Go, this is an "enclosure" type game. Being somewhat simpler, it is good practice for Gobang and the real game of Go.

For Warfare you use the board with 10 squares to a side and move only on the black squares. Each player gets 15 playing pieces, one set red, the other white. Place them on the black squares of the first 3 rows, directly opposite each other. Players move alternately, and can move diagonally in all directions, but no jumping is allowed. The object of the game is to block your opponent's pieces so they cannot move. A block normally requires 4 pieces, but a piece can be enclosed at the edge of the game board with only 2 pieces. Immobilized pieces

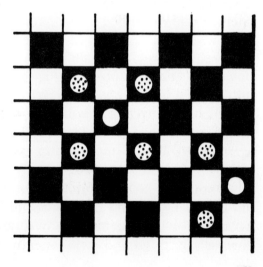

Illus. 27. In Warfare, you capture your opponent's men by blocking them so they cannot move diagonally.

are considered "captured" and removed from the board. A player must also be careful to avoid the possibility of an enclosure just before the completion of the game. The winner is the one who either captures all his opponent's men or obstructs those on the board so that they cannot be moved.

Little Boxes
(*Playing time:* about 30 minutes)

Taking turns, each player lays out a playing piece on one side of a square. Since all of the playing pieces are the same color, a player can make use of pieces previously laid down by his opponent. Whenever a player completes a box—that is, adds the fourth side around a square—he claims it as his own by placing a marker of his own color within the box. The winner is the one who possesses the most squares at the end of the game.

CIVIL WAR GAME
Green versus Lilac

This game is an eye-catching wall decoration, and since the magnetic playing pieces cling to the board, play can be interrupted and the game cleared away simply by hanging it up. The playing pieces will stay in place until you can finish your game.

The Civil War Game is another type of enclosure game. It has simple rules but is exciting to play. It calls for concentration, alertness and good planning. You can use any board with from 8 to 10 squares on a side and 28 playing pieces, so you can construct the game in any number of guises. Invent one yourself!

HOW TO PLAY

(*Playing time:* 30 minutes and up)

Green battles lilac! Your opponent must be destroyed piece by piece. Your goal is to block your opponent's men with your own in a horizontal or vertical direction, similar to Warfare. If you flank your opponent's piece on two sides you may remove that piece from the game. The winner is the one who captures all the opponent's pieces.

Each player starts with 14 pieces of one color. To start the game, each player in turn places two pieces, one to a square, on any unoccupied squares he chooses. During this first part of the game, any enclosures that happen to take place do not count—the enclosed piece cannot be removed from the board.

When all the pieces are on the board, the players take turns moving one piece at a time, one square's distance. The playing pieces can move either vertically or horizontally but jumping is not allowed. Enclosed pieces are captured and if you enclose two or even three of your opponent's pieces in one move, you may remove all of them from the board. If, however, a player

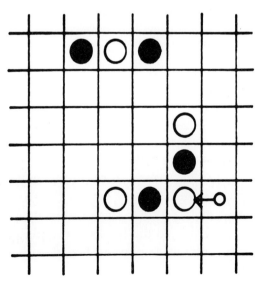

Illus. 28. The top row demonstrates a simple enclosure. In the bottom example, however, the player with the white pieces has captured two of his opponent's men with a single move.

deliberately moves one of his men between two of his opponent's pieces, this docs not count as a capture. This is an important tactical factor. It often happens a player gets so hemmed in that he cannot make a move. In this case his opponent must move and open the way for him.

HOW TO BUILD

Buy a piece of sheet metal for the board which should be about 16 inches (40 cm.) square. The metal can be thin, 18- or 20-gauge which is slightly less than $\frac{1}{16}$ inch thick (about 1 mm.). Drill a hole in each of the upper corners, so you can eventually hang the board on the wall. Scrub the sheet metal well with detergent to remove all traces of grease and spray it with several coats of colored lacquer from a spray can. Metallic finish lacquer creates a particularly decorative effect. Let the lacquer dry between coats.

With a knife and straightedge, using a cardboard base, cut 100 squares from various colors of gummed-back paper. Make the squares all a uniform size, about $1\frac{1}{4} \times 1\frac{1}{4}$ inches (3 cm. $\times$ 3 cm.). Stick them down on the lacquered sheet metal, starting in the middle and working outward. Arrange the colors in any pattern that pleases you. Leave a narrow space around each square, allowing the painted background to show through as a border. Next cut strips of gummed-back paper and stick them down around the outside of the pattern of squares to serve as a frame.

You will need 14 playing pieces in each of two different colors and these can be made from plastic tiddlywinks, coins, buttons or sections of a wood dowel. Lacquer the playing pieces in harmonizing colors. Cut a magnetic strip (available from larger office supply stores) into small squares or punch out round pieces with a paper punch. Test to see which side sticks to the sheet metal, and then use all-purpose cement to glue the non-sticking side to the backs of the playing pieces. As a final touch, spray the entire playing board with two coats of clear spraying lacquer.

Illus. 29. Build the Civil War Game out of sheet metal and fasten a magnetic strip to the back of the men so that you can hang the board on the wall with the playing pieces held in position.

Variations

You can also play the Civil War Game on a board with 8 squares to the side and 12 playing pieces per player. You can simplify construction by making all the squares the same color. Using silver squares on sheet metal sprayed with a glossy, black lacquer produces an especially attractive game board. Color the playing pieces black and red.

KUNGSER

A Tibetan Outdoor Game

Kungser, the national game of the Tibetans, belongs to the group of games widespread among many peoples, known as seige or beleaguering games. According to ethnologists, it symbolizes the centuries-long struggle between the Buddhist monks or Lamas and the Kungsers or Tibetan Princes. In the Tibetan mountains, the game would be played on a piece of bark or tree trunk, using lengths of tree branches as playing pieces. Wealthy Tibetans probably also played with precious stones on gilded game boards, while monks scratched the game board in the sand.

Our version of the game belongs outdoors, too, in the garden, on the terrace or patio. It can be left outside and a little weathering makes it even more attractive. If you have trouble locating an appropriate slice of tree trunk, ask at a lumberyard or try a sawmill if there is one nearby—they often have such blocks just lying around.

HOW TO PLAY

(*Playing time:* about 45 minutes)

Twenty-four Lamas struggle against two Princes! The Lamas' goal is to take the Princes prisoner, which they do by surrounding them so that the Princes cannot move. The Princes, for their part, try to knock out the Lamas until there are just 8 of them left. If they accomplish this, they are the victors in the struggle for power.

At the start of the game, the Princes are placed at the point of the two large quarter-circle areas, while 8 of the Lamas form a square around the empty center point.

This game proceeds in two phases. In the first, a Prince in his turn may make a move in any direction and if a Lama stands in front of him with an empty playing position beyond, the Prince can strike him down. The Lamas in opposition can use their turns to place one of their unused pieces in any empty position on the board. This is where skilful planning comes in.

The second phase begins when the 24th Lama is put on the board. All the Lamas (except those who in the meantime have been struck down and removed from the board) are now in play. They may move one space in any direction to try to encircle the Princes. The best place to do this is in the wedge-shaped areas in front of and behind the main field. The Princes continue to move or strike.

You can broaden the tactical possibilities by ruling that the Princes must strike whenever an opportunity presents itself.

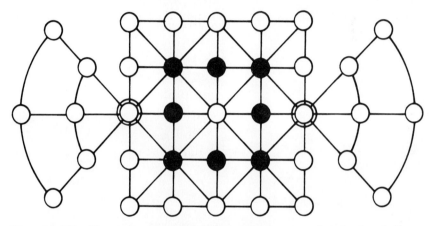

Illus. 30. The Kungser game board requires a special design following the outline above.

HOW TO BUILD

Making the Game Board

Make sure that the wood block and the branches are quite dry, and then drench all surfaces thoroughly with a penetrating wood primer. This prevents rotting and attack by vermin. Let them dry for a few days. You will need some branches about ¾ inch thick (2 cm.) and a short length about half again as thick. Paint on the game board design freehand with acrylic paint. Mark the starting positions of Lamas and Princes with brown circles.

Making the Playing Pieces

Using a mitre box, saw off 24 equal lengths from the thinner branches. Saw off two thicker pieces for the Kungsers (Princes) or mark them with some paint. Soak the pieces of branches also with wood primer.

Illus. 31. A slice of tree trunk makes a perfect game board for Kungser. Shorten or lengthen the lines to conform to the shape of the tree.

GAME CHEST
A Game Chest and Playing Table in One

This game chest is an adaptable piece of furniture. On top, you have a platform for the game boards; inside, depending on the height, you can store up to 8 game boards and their accessories. When you're not actually playing on the chest, you can use it as a side table or store it away on its side so that it takes very little space. It is a perfect piece of furniture for a dedicated game player. You can build it easily, even if you are a beginner. Just have the boards cut to size at the lumberyard.

This game box has a Far Eastern character: three of the games are from China, India and Ceylon. It is also built so low that you can sit comfortably on the floor in tailor fashion or recline like the ancient Romans. In anticipation of future additions according to your own interests, here are plans for three sheet plastic game boards, including one for Go, the fascinating Chinese game.

HOW TO BUILD

Making the Game Chest

The photo on page 53 shows how the pieces of the chest are put together. The chart below lists the materials you will need and the dimensions of each piece if you work with $\frac{3}{8}$-inch (1-cm.) plywood. The chest will accommodate 18×18 inch game boards (45×45 cm. if you use the metric specifications).

NO. OF PIECES	DIMENSIONS IN INCHES	DIMENSIONS IN CM.	PART
2	19×19	47.5×23.5	sides
1	$18\frac{1}{4} \times 19$	45.5×23.5	back
2	$18\frac{1}{4} \times 18\frac{5}{8}$	45.5×46.5	top & bottom
2	$8 \times \frac{3}{8} \times \frac{3}{8}$	$21 \times 1 \times 1$	front edging
10	$18\frac{5}{8} \times \frac{3}{4} \times \frac{3}{8}$	$46.5 \times 2 \times 1$	runners

The first step in assembling the parts is to glue the bottom between the two side pieces. When glueing, it's a good idea to tack the pieces together with small brads. Next, set the back piece between the two sides. On the inner faces of the side pieces, glue down the narrow wood strips which serve as runners for the game boards to slide on. Glue the first strip ($\frac{3}{4} \times \frac{3}{8}$ inches or 2×1 cm.) in place $\frac{3}{4}$ inch (2 cm.) down from the top to serve as a support for the top piece itself. Glue the wide side of the strip against the side wall. When you space the next runner, allow slightly more space than the thickness of your game boards for free play in moving them in and out. Continue glueing on strips until all your runners are in place. You will have some room at the bottom of the chest to store plastic boxes containing the playing pieces.

The bottom and top boards fit right inside the side and back walls. At the front edge of the top piece, glue the two edging strips each butted up against a side, leaving a space between them. This will allow you to get your fingers underneath the game boards so you can lift them out when you want to change.

Sandpaper the chest and give it two coats of lacquer. You might want to lacquer the top in a contrasting color. Sand the lacquered surfaces between the runners so that they are very smooth. Otherwise, they will scratch the sheet plastic game boards as you slip them in and out.

Cut your sheet plastic game boards to size (or buy them ready-cut) and use a grease pencil that will wipe off later to draw the playing lines onto one side of the clear sheets. On the reverse side, following the grease pencil design, press down some strips of masking tape to outline where you want to paint the horizontal lines. Paint them on with colored lacquer. Let the paint dry, remove the masking tape, and do the same with the vertical lines.

Make one board with 19×19 lines for Go, another with 10 squares to a side for Reversi, Warfare, Civil War and Cops & Robber; and a third with the special board for the Sixteen Soldiers Game.

Slip the boards into their grooves, fill small plastic boxes

Illus. 32. The game chest not only serves as a platform for the board in use, but provides slots to hold additional boards and space to store the various kinds of playing pieces.

with 200 chips each of two different colors and place them in the bottom compartment.

HOW TO PLAY

Sixteen Soldiers Game

(*Playing time:* 40 minutes and up)

This game is popular in India and Ceylon. Two armies battle each other, with the goal of destroying the opposing force. The starting positions for the two groups of 16 pieces and the layout of the game board are shown in Illus. 33. A soldier may jump over an enemy playing piece and remove it from the board, so long as there is an empty playing position

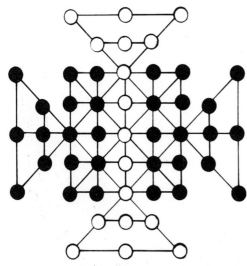

Illus. 33. This is the outline of the board for the Sixteen Soldiers Game. The black circles indicate the starting positions of the players.

behind it. Otherwise, the players take turns, moving one position in any direction. Jumping over more than one opposing player in a move is not allowed. Players can make use of the side wings of the game board for evasive action.

The winner of the game is the first player to reduce the opposing force to two soldiers.

Cows and Leopards

(*Playing time:* about 50 minutes)

Also from Ceylon, this siege game is similar to Kungser. Twenty-four cows have to defend themselves against two leopards. The game is played on the same board as the Sixteen Soldiers Game. One player takes the part of the leopards, the other that of the cows. The cows try to hem in the leopards so they can make no more moves. The leopards try to do away with the cows—that is, remove them from the board by jumping over them. This is allowed only when a cow stands in front of a leopard and there is an empty playing space directly behind it. The cows cannot eliminate the leopards, but due to their superior number try to win by encircling the leopards, hemming them in so they can make no further moves.

Start with an empty board. The leopard player begins by placing a leopard on any position he wishes. The cow player then places a cow on whatever position he thinks best. His opponent puts down the second leopard. For the following turns, the leopards can move in any direction, but the cow player, instead of moving, must continue to place cows on the board, until all of them (except for those which the leopards strike from the board) are in play. Only then are cows allowed to move, one space in any direction. The leopards must remove all 16 cows to win. The cows win if they succeed in surrounding the leopards so they cannot move.

Go

(Playing time: 60 minutes and up)

The ancient Chinese game of Go has been called the most ingenious of all board games because of its logical structure

Illus. 34. This game chest has been finished with stain and lacquer. The game in progress is Go.

and abundance of possibilities for using tactics—even more so than chess. The basic rules of Go are simple and easy to learn.

Go was mentioned in Chinese literature as early as the 17th century, B.C. From China, it spread to Japan, to the palaces of the emperor and the royal princes. For hundreds of years the Japanese maintained a government "Go Academy." Even today there are professional Go teachers, and 10 million active players in Japan alone.

Introduced to the West in the 20th century, the game quickly became popular. Most large cities have "Go Societies" whose members play regularly.

Another enclosure game, Go surpasses all the rest with its enormous number of combination possibilities and tactical refinements. The following paragraphs give the fundamental rules of the game. If you enjoy playing Go, you can proceed to learn its finer points from some of the whole books that have been written about the game.

The Go board has 19 horizontal and 19 vertical lines which cross each other at right angles, creating 361 points of play. Unlike most board games, which are played on the squares, Go is played on the crosspoints of the lines. Each player receives 180 playing pieces (plastic chips) of one color.

It is much easier to learn Go if you start by playing on a smaller game board, one, for example, that has 10 squares to a side, which creates 11 × 11 crosspoints or 121 points of play. You will want to include such a board in your game box for some of the games such as Reversi described earlier. In this beginning game, each player starts with 50 chips. Each player in turn places one piece on any crosspoint. Once put down, the pieces are never moved. The darker color (red in the photograph) always begins.

You have two goals: first, to enclose your opponent's playing pieces, causing them to be removed from play, and, second, to "fence in" and control as large an area of the game board as possible. At the end of the game, each opposing player you have enclosed and every unoccupied crosspoint within the areas you control will count one point in your favor.

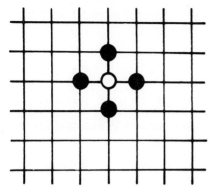

Illus. 35. In this example, four red pieces have enclosed a single white piece.

Illus. 36. Here, three red pieces have been enclosed by white playing pieces.

To enclose an opponent's piece, you must surround it on all sides. Enclosed pieces are "dead" and removed from the board. For examples, see Illus. 35 where red has a white piece enclosed and Illus. 36 where white has three red pieces enclosed.

Illus. 37 shows another kind of encirclement. Here the enclosed pieces are not considered "dead" because there are still some empty crosspoints, called "eyes," inside the enclosed area. The red pieces in this example are considered "captured" and not removed from the board. In such a situation, there is still a chance that they will be freed if the chain holding them in can be "broken," that is, if additional red pieces can be put down in turn to enclose some of the encircling white pieces causing their removal from the board.

Illus. 37. The red pieces in this example are enclosed but they cannot be removed from the board since there are still some empty crosspoints within the enclosed area.

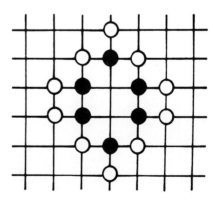

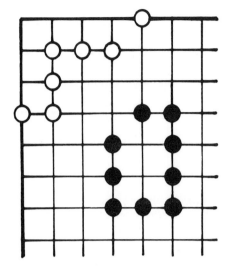

Illus. 38. One of the goals in playing Go is to fence in as much territory as possible by constructing barriers along the edges or enclosures in the middle of the board.

In enclosing an area, the object is to block off a space containing as many empty crosspoints as possible. In Illus. 38, white has occupied the upper left-hand corner of the playing board. The enclosing line must be without gaps. Red has occupied a circular area. Every empty crosspoint within these enclosed areas is worth one point when it is time to count up the score. It would be senseless for a player to put down one of his pieces within an area he has already enclosed, and it is not allowed, except when a player can thereby enclose an opponent's playing piece that is holding some of his own men captive. You must, of course, try to prevent your opponent from constructing barriers and enclosures. In doing this, you must sometimes put your own men down in territory that has been enclosed already by your opponent. Such men are not "dead," only "captured." Making enclosures along the edges of the playing field is usually a good tactic.

Another important rule called "Ko" applies to "killing" pieces. Look at Illus. 39. In this example, white has just killed a red piece. The last played white piece is the one with dots inside the circle. The red piece to the right will be removed from the board as in Illus. 40. Theoretically, red could "strike back" now by putting a piece on the just-vacated eye, killing the last-played white piece. This type of move is forbidden, however,

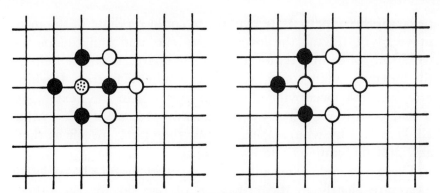

Illus. 39 and 40. The rule called "Ko" forbids a player from playing a piece on the spot from which one of his men has just been removed, until the next following move.

as it would lead to a chain of alternating moves of the same kind, which would be pointless. Red is not allowed to "strike back" in this manner until the next following move, which gives white the opportunity in the meantime to cover the threatening crosspoint with one of his own pieces.

One more important rule is called "Seki." It applies to the situation where in an enclosing manoeuvre, each player, the conqueror as well as the victim, would lose his pieces. In this case the manoeuvre is declared a tie. Look at Illus. 41 where neither white nor red can make an attack. Were red to set a

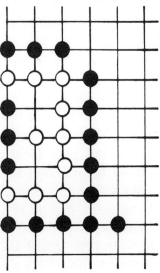

Illus. 41. The rule called "Seki" applies to this situation where neither white nor red can make an attack.

piece on the upper empty eye, white could retaliate in the next move by occupying the lower empty eye, and four red pieces would be killed and removed from the board. With the help of the free eyes, white could build an unassailable fortress. If white attacked first, occupying the lower eye, red in the next move would occupy the other eye which would result in the loss of all 11 pieces by white. "Seki" areas, therefore, are left as they are, and the game continues elsewhere.

The game ends when all the crosspoints inside the enclosed areas are clearly in the possession of one side or the other. Players usually put down their last remaining pieces in neutral zones—this doesn't win any points but it makes counting up easier.

The final step of the game of Go is the settlement. Count up your opponent's killed and captured pieces and add this to the number of empty crosspoints remaining within the areas your pieces have enclosed. The empty crosspoints inside a Seki-area do not add points to either side. The player with the most points wins.

With these ground rules, you are ready to look for a Go match. It takes some time, naturally, to become an accomplished player. The best thing to do is to get some instructions in the fine points of the game from good players.

Gobang
(*Playing time:* 40 minutes and up)

Gobang is less complicated to play than Go, but you still need to think cleverly to win. It is good preliminary practice for Go.

You can play Gobang on the full-size Go board or on a smaller board, such as the 10 × 10 square board (11 × 11 lines) contained in the game box. Like Go, Gobang is played not on the squares, but on the crosspoints of the lines.

Give each player 60 to 100 chips of one color, depending on the size of the board and whether you want to play for a longer or shorter time. Then, taking turns, set your pieces down on any crosspoints on the board. The goal of each side is to build a closed row of 5 playing pieces in a horizontal, vertical, or diagonal direction. At the same time, of course, you want to prevent your opponent from building one. The first player to complete a row of five pieces is the winner and the game is over.

If it should happen that all the pieces are put down and still no row has been formed, the already-played pieces are "set free," that is, at each turn you may pick up any one of your pieces and relocate it elsewhere on some other crosspoint. This goes on until some player succeeds in completing a row of 5 pieces.

Experienced Gobang players try to set their playing pieces in the form of a cross so that their opponent is forced to defend himself in more places while giving themselves more chances for completing a row.

If you play Gobang with 3 or 4 players, give each player 20–30 pieces.

Games for Two
or More Players

Playing with a larger group? Then the next games are especially suitable.

Set up an evening of games with your family and friends. To enjoy it fully, plan it as you would a dinner menu, with hors d'oeuvres, main dish and dessert. Get the evening started with a short warm-up game which is not too difficult. For a "main dish," serve up a longer, more difficult game, and, towards the end of the evening, when excited minds need calming down, you can relax with something light.

Your whole family can play these games, and it's even more fun to get everyone to work together on construction. Let everyone join in—and get your game ready for a rainy Sunday. You will be amazed at how many ideas for new games and new game rules will result!

VOCABULARY AND KNOWLEDGE GAMES
Who Is Best Informed?

Both of these games will develop your vocabulary and increase your knowledge.

HOW TO PLAY

Word Track
(*Playing time:* 60 minutes and up)

The game board is made up of 5 tracks with differently colored backgrounds. Each player takes one of the playing pieces that is colored to match the tracks, to serve as his runner. In addition, each player chooses one of the flat round pieces marked with letters of the alphabet that have been turned face down. Each player turns his letter face up in the center field of his own track and places his runner in starting

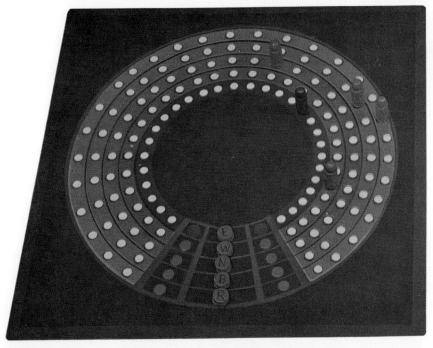

Illus. 42. Choose bright colors to set off the Word Track game to best advantage.

position—just to the right of his letter. The player on the inside track starts first and must name a word which contains the letter he has drawn as many times as possible, but the word should not contain *any* of the letters belonging to his opponents. For example, in the game in Illus. 42, Blue's letter is "e," and his word should not contain w, n, b or r. He could say "see" and then move forward (counter-clockwise) two playing positions, since his word contains two "e's." If he said, "somewhere," he could move forward three playing positions (his word has three "e's"), but the players who drew the "r" and the "w" could also move forward one square each.

Each player must call out a word right away when his turn comes up; if he can't, he loses his turn. It's a good idea, therefore, to think up your next word while your opponents are busy with their moves. Again, try not to include other players' letters in your word. Any player who speaks out of turn has to move back 5 spaces! The first player to reach the other end of the circular track wins.

You can make the game more difficult by making it a rule that only special categories of words can be chosen—only verbs, or adjectives, or words from specific fields, such as geography or medicine, or only words from a foreign language if all players know or are studying it.

Word Race
(*Playing time:* 60 minutes and up)

This game tests your general knowledge. Make a deck of category cards by writing on them such things as: A Kind of Sport, A Famous Person in History, A Geographical Feature, A Profession, A Chemical Element, A Country, A Disease or Illness, An Animal, etc. Place the cards face down on the rectangle at the right of the game board. (See Illus. 43.)

Each player chooses a runner and puts it down on the starting circle in the track of the same color. The player to the right begins. On the game board in Illus. 43, the letter "a" is just ahead. The player takes the top card from the pile. It may say, for example, "Famous Person of Antiquity." The answer may be Aristotle (or Archimedes, Alexander the Great, Alaric—any name that starts with "A"). Moving his runner forward one step to the next letter, the player puts the used card on the rectangle on the other side of the track. The next player takes the top card from the right pile, and the game proceeds.

Answers must be given within a predetermined amount of time. A player who cannot think of an answer in time must move back one playing square and repeat the letter he previously completed when his next turn comes up. When a player completes the first loop, he comes to the center crossing and the "difficult letters."

Before play begins, pick out the hard letters such as q, v, x and z from the marked set of playing pieces, mix them up and place them face down in the middle section of the track. As each player arrives at the center crossing, he uncovers the letter on his track and tries to give a word according to the card he turns over. He may not move on until he can come up with an answer, but if he cannot think of one, he does not have to move back. He draws a different card on his next turn and tries again to supply a word starting with the letter in his track. When he succeeds, he may move on and the winner is the player who reaches the end of his track first.

Variations

You can shorten the game by playing only up to the crossing between loops. In another short version of the game, a player may move forward one letter for each name he can think of in the category on the card within a specified period of time. Other variations can be thought up for both boards so that they need never become boring.

Making the Tracks

For either board you start with a piece of plywood about 16 × 16 inches square (40 × 40 cm.). Paint over the entire board with wood paint of the background color. Using a compass, ruler and lead pencil, lightly draw in the pattern of

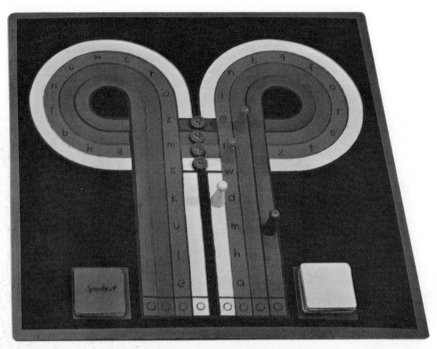

Illus. 43. Use the brightest color for the outside track, to serve as an outline for the Word Race game.

the playing field. You can draw the pattern on paper first, if you wish, then transfer it to the board with carbon paper. Paint the tracks in their various colors and, when they are dry, paint dark lines between them. If you have a steady hand, you can work freehand, but choose a good quality fine-line brush for this delicate work. Handpainted game boards have enormous charm!

Making the Playing Pieces

Mark 26 plastic tiddlywinks or sections cut from a wooden dowel so that each shows a different letter of the alphabet. Use a soft-tip ink marker with indelible colored ink. Cut out little cards from some stiff board stock and write the legends on them, also with a soft-tip ink marker. A few more examples of categories are: City, River, Occupation, Fish, Play, Opera—you will think of many more. The runners can also be made from dowels, drawer pulls or other interestingly shaped pieces of wood. Paint them with colors that match the tracks they occupy. Finally, give the playing pieces and game board surfaces a sealing coat of clear lacquer. If you paint with acrylic tube colors, use a clear coat of matt (or glossy) medium.

Illus. 44. This is the pegboard box described on the following pages. You can use wooden dowels for the pegs or, as shown here, a metal rod with pointed ends provides an attractive alternative.

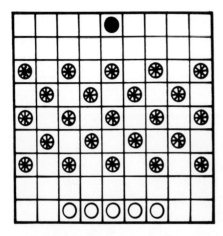

Illus. 45. This is the starting position for Cops and Robber.

A BOXFUL OF PEGBOARD GAMES
A Colorful Mixture for Brainy People

This box with its colorful pegs is a job for the experienced home craftsman. You can hang it on the wall and change the color pattern continually by moving the pegs around. Of course, you can also play many games with it.

The box contains a drawer that pulls out in which you can keep the game rules and playing pieces. In the box pictured, the playing pins or pegs were cut from aluminum rod, but pegs made from hardwood dowel will work just as well.

HOW TO PLAY

Cops and Robber (for two players)
(*Playing time:* about 20 minutes)

The hunt for the robber takes place in a forest. Five policemen try to catch a thief. Place 23 green and blue pegs in the middle rows of the board, with an empty hole between them (see Illus. 45). This is the forest. Five cops, red-painted pegs, are placed in the first row on one side of the woods; the robber, one of the yellow pegs, is on the other side. The cops can move one space at a time either forward or sideways; the robber can also make these moves, and he can move one space backward as well. To escape, he has to reach the other side of the woods, "slipping through the fingers of the law," so to speak. If he accomplishes this, he is the winner. If he is not clever enough, the cops will surround him so that he cannot make another move. In this case, the police win. Players must move around the trees, not jump over them, but the robber can jump diagonally over a policeman if the playing position behind him is unoccupied.

Place-Changing Game (for 2 or 4 players)
(*Playing time:* about 60 minutes)

Each player receives 9 pegs of one color and places them in the corner holes as shown in Illus. 46. Your goal is to take possession of the opposite side of the board in the shortest time possible. You can move forward, sideways, or diagonally, but not backward. You can jump over your own players as well as your opponents' in order to move forward faster.

Variations

Decide, before you begin to play, whether you want to play "peaceably" or "aggressively." In a peaceable game, you may jump over your opponents' men, but leave them on the board. In an aggressive game, when you jump them, you remove them from play. The first one to get all his pegs to the other side of the board wins.

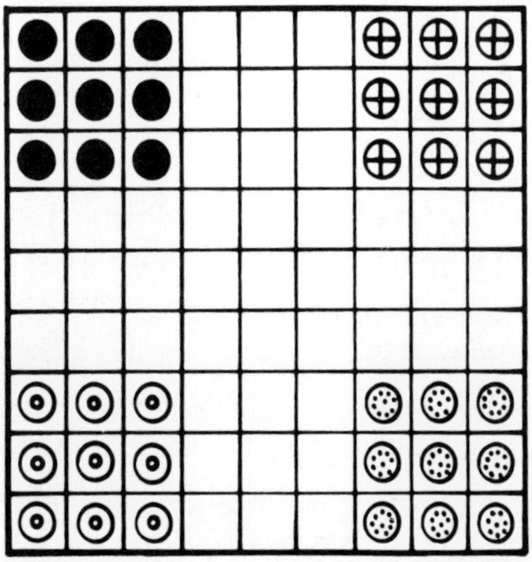

Illus. 46. Here are the starting positions for the Place-Changing Game. With only two players, begin with the playing pieces in diagonally opposite corners.

When only two people play, you can set up additional obstacles by putting in some barriers made up of the other color pegs not in play. See Illus. 47 for some suggestions. Skilful players can turn these obstacles to their own advantage.

Other games that you can play on your pegboard are Civil War, Gobang, and simple Go.

HOW TO BUILD
Making the Peg Box

You will need the following material:

NO. OF PIECES	DIMENSIONS IN INCHES	DIMENSIONS IN CM.	PART
$\frac{3}{8}''$ (1 cm.) *plywood*			
1	14×14	35×35	pegboard
2	$14 \times 2\frac{1}{2}$	35×6	box sides
2	$14\frac{3}{8} \times 2\frac{1}{2}$	36×6	box back drawer front
3	$13\frac{3}{8} \times 1\frac{1}{2}$	33.5×4	drawer sides and divider
1	$13\frac{3}{4} \times 1\frac{1}{2}$	34.5×4	drawer back
$\frac{1}{4}''$ (.4 cm.) *plywood*			
1	14×14	35×35	support board
1	$14\frac{3}{4} \times 14\frac{3}{8}$	37×36	box bottom
1	$13\frac{3}{4} \times 13\frac{3}{4}$	34.5×34.5	drawer bottom
$\frac{1}{2}''$ (1.2 cm.) *wooden dowel*			
81	2	5	playing pieces

To begin, glue the box back and sides to the bottom board. Drill 81 holes (9 rows of 9 holes each) in the thick plywood square that is to serve as the pegboard. Test your drill bit first in a piece of scrap wood to be sure the dowels fit smoothly into the hole it makes. Glue the pegboard to the support board which serves as a stop for the pegs.

Next, glue the drawer sides and the divider to the drawer bottom. When the drawer dries, put it inside the still-open box.

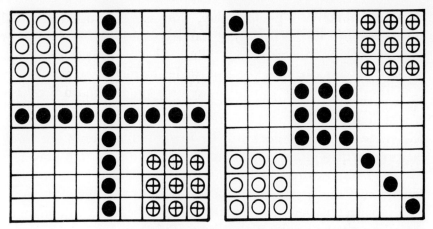

Illus. 47. To make the Place-Changing Game more difficult when there are only two players, set up some additional obstacles of the other color pegs not in play.

Lay the pegboard in place through the open top of the box and mark where it should be glued, allowing a little extra space above the drawer for free movement. This should be about $\frac{1}{8}$ inch (3 mm.). Glue the top in place.

Finally, drill a finger hole in the middle of the drawer front and glue it to the drawer so that it lines up with the sides of the chest.

Using your mitre box, cut 81 2-inch (5-cm.) lengths of dowel and sand the ends smooth.

Paint the box, drawer and playing pieces black. When they are dry, apply a coat of clear brushing lacquer. Paint the round ends of the pegs using four different, contrasting colors. You will have an extra peg of one color but it's a good idea to make a few extra of each color. You'll need them to replace lost pieces. When they are dry, apply a coat of clear brushing lacquer.

Write the rules of the games in a small notebook and place it in the box. To hang the peg box on the wall, drive two nails into the back of the box and stretch a piece of picture wire between them. Be sure to arrange it so that the drawer side faces up!

REVOLUTION
A Decorative Pattern for Your Wall and a Game Too

This project has been put at the end of the book because in its construction, as well as in its playing, it demands the qualities of the really dedicated game fan—patience, perseverance, precision and skill. It takes more than one evening to construct this game but your effort will be rewarded not only with an exciting tactical game which can be played by up to 6 players, but also by an attractive, decorative object. Hang it on the wall and change the arrangement of the designs and colors to suit your mood. The pattern of shadows and reflections will change according to the angle of the light. This is a "game picture" or "picture game" in the truest sense of the word. Even while you play, the varying form and color combinations which evolve make the game a pleasure for your eyes as well as a challenge to your mind.

Revolution consists of 100 blocks or cubes all decorated alike with a different color and/or design on each of their 6 faces. Some of the design elements are cut out of gleaming metal

Illus. 48. Construct the Revolution game so that you can slide a piece of sheet plastic over the top of the blocks, allowing you to hang it on the wall without the cubes falling out.

foil and glued to the surface, others are simply painted on and lacquered over. As a result, when light plays on the pieces, it creates an enormous variety of strong and weak reflections. The cubes are not difficult to make—but you do need patience because there is quite a lot of painting involved. The box, on the other hand, calls for precise workmanship. It has a slide-on cover of sheet plastic, and a small compartment for each cube, made of crisscrossed strips of wood. These compartments make it easier to put the blocks into play and it keeps them from all sliding together when you hang the box on the wall.

HOW TO PLAY

(*Playing time:* depending on number of players, 60 minutes or more)

The game is a further development of Reversi, described in an earlier section. Any number of players from 2 to 6 can join in the game.

The 6 sides of each cube are decorated as follows: solid blue, solid red, a red dot on a blue field, a blue dot on a red field, a green dot on a turquoise field, a silver square on a blue field. Each player chooses one of the sides as his color.

The cubes are distributed according to the number of players, with any left-over cubes put aside:

2 players—50 cubes each
3 players—33 cubes each
4 players—25 cubes each
5 players—20 cubes each
6 players—16 cubes each

The players proceed in turn, each setting out one cube at a time, with his color up, on any unoccupied square on the playing board. The goal is to enclose one or more of an opponent's cubes with two of your own cubes in a vertical, horizontal, or diagonal direction. The enclosed cubes are then turned over so that they show the encloser's color on top. These "overturned" blocks now belong to the player who has captured

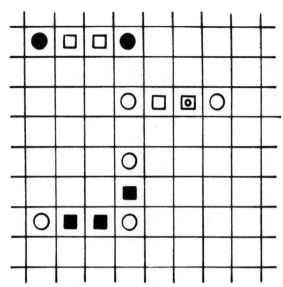

Illus. 49. An enclosure is valid only if the enclosed cubes belong to one opponent as in the examples at the top and bottom. Mixed pieces as in the middle do not count.

them. This does not mean that they cannot change sides again, if some other player succeeds in enclosing them again. An enclosure is effective only when all the enclosed cubes belong to one opponent—"mixed" sides do not count.

In Illus. 49, for example, the black circles in the top group of playing pieces have enclosed two white squares, and that player can turn them over to show his own face side up. In the middle group of pieces, the white circles have enclosed cubes of two different opponents, and this does not count. If a player can set out a cube which makes two enclosures, he may take advantage of both of them. In the bottom group of figures, the last play was the white circle set out in the corner position. With this one move, he enclosed both the vertical and the horizontal black square pieces. Enclosures that appear as captured pieces are turned over do not count. This is a game that rewards advance planning carried out over many moves, especially around the corners!

You can play other games on this board, too—such as Salta, Warfare, and Civil War.

Illus. 50. When your game is not in use, it makes an attractive, colorful display. Turning over a few blocks can completely change the balance and mood of the composition.

HOW TO BUILD
Making the Box

The exact dimensions of the box depend upon what size blocks you use and the size of the wood strips that will serve as partitions to mark off the compartments. The job goes much faster if you use a small, ready-made molding for these dividers rather than trying to cut your own strips.

Use $\frac{3}{8}$-inch thick (1-cm.) plywood for the bottom of the box, using a pencil and ruler to divide the board into squares. You have to allow for the thickness of the cubes which will be about 1 inch (2.5 cm.), the width of the divider strips which should be about $\frac{1}{4}$ inch (6 mm.), and some extra space to allow free movement of the blocks—about $\frac{1}{16}$ inch (2 mm.) on each side. If you use these exact dimensions, your bottom board will measure 14×14 inches (35.6×35.6 cm.).

Cut 11 of the divider strips the length of the bottom board and attach them, all running in one direction. To obtain exactly the right separation between the strips, saw off a piece of spacer board equal to the width of the cube and the space you are allowing for movement on each side—in the case above, $1\frac{1}{8}$ inch (2.9 cm.). Glue the first strip flush with the edge of the bottom board and use your spacer to place the next strip. You can use small brads to hold the strips in place while the glue dries but tack them in alongside the strips rather than through them to avoid splitting the wood. Just tack them in a little ways so you can pull them out easily when the glue dries.

Next come the short cross pieces to complete the compartments. You will need 110 of them the same length as your spacer. Again start flush at one of the edges of the board and proceed using a spacer to maintain the exact distance. When all the glue is dry, remove the brads and sand the whole board smooth.

The frame of the box is made from lengths of $\frac{3}{4}$-inch thick (2-cm.) boards. Calculate their height by adding up the thickness of the bottom board, the width of the cubes, the thickness of the piece of sheet plastic you will use as a cover plus an allowance of $\frac{1}{16}$ inch (2 mm.) between the cube faces and the cover and another $\frac{1}{4}$ inch (6 mm.) as a frame above the cover. This will add up to about 2 inches (5 cm.). Three of the faces need to have a groove cut in them to serve as a slide for the sheet plastic cover. Alternatively, you can glue some lengths of the same strips you used as dividers to serve as supports above and below the cover. The front, the still-open side of the box, calls for a wood strip that is just high enough to reach from the bottom of the base to the bottom of the grooves in the sides. Cut a wooden spacer slightly thicker than the sheet plastic cover and on top of the spacers fasten a thin strip of wood to complete the top frame.

Sand the whole box thoroughly and apply two coats of satin-finish lacquer or varnish. Smooth the finish between coats with fine sandpaper.

Making the Playing Pieces

Cut the 100 wooden blocks from lengths of ready-made square molding. Use an acrylic wood finish to paint on the background colors—three sides a powerful blue, two sides carmine red, and one side turquoise blue. Using a cardboard pattern or some round object like a small bottle cap or a coin, trace the outline of a circle on one of the blue sides of each cube. Paint the inside of the circle red with a fine brush. Similarly, trace 100 circles on blue and green metal-foil paper and cut them out. Glue the green circles to the turquoise-blue faces of the cubes, the blue ones to a red face, applying the adhesive thinly. Next, fasten squares cut from silver-colored metal-foil paper to one of the blue sides of the cubes. In preparing the cube faces, try to arrange it so that the various faces are in the same relationship to one another, so that in playing, the players do not have to spend too much time hunting for their own colors when turning cubes over.

When all the sides are finished, give the cubes a coat of clear brushing lacquer (or acrylic glossy medium if you used acrylic tube colors).

Test the finish first on a piece of scrap metal foil as many lacquers attack or corrode this material. Allow several hours for everything to dry thoroughly.

When you have arrived at this point, there is nothing left except to wish you many hours of enjoyment with your new games!

Illus. 51. Revolution, like all of the games in this book, is meant to be enjoyed when not in use as well as be fun to make and play. You can hang the games on the wall or display them on a table.

Solutions to Puzzles

THE TURNCOATS: GAME I

3 — 4	2 — 4	7 — 5	3 — 2
5 — 3	1 — 2	6 — 7	5 — 3
6 — 5	3 — 1	4 — 6	4 — 5
4 — 6	5 — 3	2 — 4	

THE TURNCOATS: GAME 2

F — E	F — H	G — E	C — B
D — F	D — F	I — G	E — C
C — D	B — D	H — I	G — E
E — C	A — B	F — H	F — G
G — E	C — A	D — F	D — F
H — G	E — C	B — D	E — D

SOLITAIRE: GAME I

5 — 17	13 — 11	20 — 18	33 — 25	25 — 23	7 — 9
12 — 10	18 — 6	18 — 30	31 — 33	28 — 16	9 — 23
3 — 11	3 — 11	27 — 25	18 — 30	21 — 23	14 — 16
1 — 3	30 — 18	30 — 18	33 — 25	16 — 28	17 — 15
10 — 12	11 — 25	28 — 30	16 — 28	4 — 16	28 — 16
					15 — 17

SOLITAIRE: GAME 2

19 — 17	29 — 17	22 — 24	3 — 11	13 — 27	27 — 25
16 — 18	18 — 16	30 — 18	18 — 6	1 — 3	3 — 11
14 — 16	16 — 14	27 — 25	10 — 8	21 — 7	7 — 9
5 — 17	12 — 10	31 — 23	16 — 28	33 — 31	31 — 23
17 — 15	4 — 16	7 — 9	24 — 26		

SOLITAIRE: GAME 3

5 — 17	1 — 9	3 — 11	16 — 28	24 — 26
8 — 10	10 — 8	7 — 9	14 — 16	32 — 24
1 — 9	11 — 3	24 — 10	31 — 23	27 — 25
3 — 1	13 — 11	28 — 16	26 — 24	20 — 18
16 — 4	18 — 6	21 — 23	33 — 25	

SOLITAIRE: GAME 4

3 — 1	4 — 6	5 — 18	34 — 32	23 — 25
12 — 2	18 — 5	33 — 20	20 — 33	18 — 31
8 — 6	20 — 18	29 — 27	18 — 31	19 — 32
20 — 7	1 — 11	20 — 33	16 — 18	36 — 26
15 — 13	6 — 19	22 — 20	35 — 25	30 — 32
7 — 20	18 — 5	37 — 27	33 — 31	26 — 36
2 — 12	9 — 11	31 — 33	25 — 35	35 — 37

Index